Collins English

Series editors: F

A library of graded r
reluctant native reac
Structure, vocabula
principles laid down
books are listed belc
words and appropriac

MW00979895

5: 2000 words and 6: 2500 words. Those titles which are asterisked are
accompanied by a cassette.

Level Four

The White South *Hammond Innes*
A Christmas Carol *Charles Dickens*
King Solomon's Mines*
H Rider Haggard
Jane Eyre *Charlotte Brontë*
Pride and Prejudice *Jane Austen*
Dr Jekyll and Mr Hyde*
R L Stevenson
Huckleberry Finn *Mark Twain*
Landslide *Desmond Bagley*
Nothing is the Number When You
Die *Joan Fleming*
The African Child *Camara Laye*
The Lovely Lady and other Stories
D H Lawrence
Airport International *Brian Moynahan*
The Secret Sharer and other Sea
Stories *Joseph Conrad*
Death in Vienna? *K E Rowlands*
Hostage Tower* *Alistair MacLean*
The Potter's Wheel *Chukwuemeka Ike*
Tina Turner *Stephen Rabley*
Campbell's Kingdom *Hammond Innes*
Barchester Towers *Anthony Trollope*
Rear Window *Cornell Woolrich*

Level Five

The Guns of Navarone
Alistair MacLean

Geordie *David Walker*
Wuthering Heights *Emily Brontë*
Where Eagles Dare *Alistair MacLean*
Wreck of the Mary Deare
Hammond Innes
I Know My Love *Catherine Gaskin*
The Mayor of Casterbridge
Thomas Hardy
Sense and Sensibility *Jane Austen*
The Eagle has Landed *Jack Higgins*
Middlemarch *George Eliot*
Victory *Joseph Conrad*
Experiences of Terror* *Roland John*
Japan: Islands in the Mist
Peter Milward
The Freedom Trap *Desmond Bagley*

Level Six

Doctor Zhivago *Boris Pasternak*
The Glory Boys *Gerald Seymour*
In the Shadow of Man *Jane Goodall*
Harry's Game *Gerald Seymour*
House of a Thousand Lanterns
Victoria Holt
Hard Times *Charles Dickens*
Sons and Lovers *D H Lawrence*
The Dark Frontier *Eric Ambler*
Vanity Fair *William Thackeray*
Inspector Ghote Breaks an Egg
H R F Keating

NELSON MANDELA

ADRIENNE SWINDELLS

CollinsELT

A Division of HarperCollins*Publishers*

Copyright © HarperCollins Publishers Ltd, 1991

Published in Great Britain by
Collins ELT
HarperCollins Publishers
77–85 Fulham Palace Road
London W6 8JB

Printed in Great Britain by Martin's of Berwick

First published in the Collins English Library, 1991

ISBN 0 00 370736 9

We are grateful to Popperfoto/Reuter for
permission to reproduce the photograph which
appears on the cover and to IDAF for permission to
use those in the text.

The Collins English Library grading system has
made it necessary to simplify many of the
quotations used in this book. Every effort has been
made to retain the spirit of the words quoted.

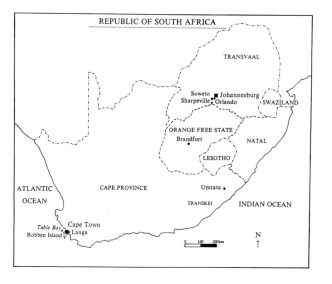

"I fought against white rule and
I fought against black rule.
I dreamed of a land which belongs
to all the people. A land where all
men live in peace and are equal.
It is a dream I hope to live for.
But if necessary, it is a dream
I am ready to die for."

EARLY DAYS
1918–1940

'I would like to take you away from everything, out into the beauty that is South Africa. Where the flowers grow wild and the trees are green. Where animals follow the river bed and where people have time to stand and talk,' wrote Nelson to Winnie from Robben Island in 1976.

ALONE IN PRISON AT NIGHT, Nelson often thought of his early life in the Transkei. He remembered how he followed the animals and worked in the fields. He remembered the white washed home where he lived. There was a place to cook, a place to sleep and a place to keep the food.

The home where Nelson lived as a child

Rolihlahla Nelson Mandela was born near Umtata, on 18 July 1918. He was the son of the third wife of Henry Mandela. On his death bed, his father sent for ten year old Nelson. "I have no money to leave to you," he told the young boy. "But you needn't worry, you will be taken care of by the leader of the Thembu people, the Chief himself. He will decide your future."

It was the beginning of a new life for Nelson. There was no more working on the land or wearing his father's old clothes. He was sent to school and taken into the Chief's comfortable home.

'I was his child now,' Nelson wrote. *'Part of his family. It was kind of him but not at all unusual. It's what you do for your own people.'* In later years, Nelson's own home was always open to family.

The schoolboy Nelson became interested in the story of South Africa's past. At night under a starry African sky he listened to the old chiefs. There were stories exciting enough for any growing child. Stories of battles lost and won. And stories of the lands which belonged to the black man until the white man came along.

Years later, Nelson said, "I grew up with the stories of the past, when the land was ours. In those days there were no rich and poor, and all men were free and equal. And I learned too how this changed – how the white man came and took what was not his.

But, worst of all, I learned that the white man hated the black."

The young Nelson found out that the white man still hated the black man. In the white man's eyes, the black man was no better than a wild animal. The books in Nelson's school said the white man knew everything. The black man knew only how to cause trouble. Nelson wondered how one man could write that about another. *He* knew it was untrue, why didn't everybody else? He worked hard at school. And he tried to forget the books which said unfair things about the black man.

In 1938, Nelson went to college, and with this came the fun of student life.

"We were good-looking and all the women wanted us." To make the most of themselves, Nelson and a friend learned to dance. Dressed in their black suits and ties, they broke college rules and went to the nearest dance hall.

She looked and danced like a film star. Nelson held her closer. "What's your name?" he asked. His mind was busy planning their next meeting.

"Mrs Bokwe," she told him. Two college teachers were staring at him from the edge of the dance floor.

Nelson was sent home from college. Not for dancing with Mr Bokwe's wife, but for refusing to eat college food.

"You must return, at once," the Chief told

him angrily. "You must say you're sorry and get back to work. That is why you're at college, not to argue about the food."

"I loved him," said Nelson. "I didn't want to hurt him, so I decided to go back. But when I was ready to leave, he came to talk to me."

"I have a surprise for you," he said. "Your future wife is here to meet you. The marriage is fixed – the day, the date, and, of course, the price."

Nelson aged nineteen

"But . . . but . . . I don't know her. I'm not ready to get married yet. And when I am, I shall choose my own wife." Nelson tried not to be angry.

But the Chief wasn't listening and would never listen.

"I knew I was no better than a clockwork dog," said Nelson. "He turned the key and I ran round."

That night with the help of his cousin, Nelson stole two animals and sold them. With the money they ran away.

LAND OF PROMISE

THE WHITE MAN FOUND RICHES beyond his wildest dreams in South Africa. There was land to be farmed and gold to be dug from the mines. And there were people, eight million of them, all black, to work the land and dig the mines.

Almost overnight the white man was rich. Soon, he wanted to be richer. He wanted more land, more mines, more money. And he wanted to make sure that it would be his for ever.

The number of blacks was growing much faster than the whites in South Africa. The white man was frightened. He talked a lot about "black danger". The idea grew until most whites believed that the black man was their enemy, and must be kept down.

In 1910, there were thirty-six rules which stopped a man enjoying a full life because he was black. The whites had all the power, and in 1936 they changed the law. From now on, the black man could not even decide who ruled him. He had no voice at all in choosing a government.

Millions of blacks were forced from their homes to live in the worst parts of the cities. From there they went to work for the white man, who paid them as little as possible.

Now the white man worried that there were too many black people almost on his own doorstep. To feel really safe, he wanted to know everything about the black man. Where he was, and what he was doing, every minute of the day and night.

He could think of only one way to do it – Pass Laws. By law, everybody must carry a written pass. "Everybody", of course, meant the black people. By 1936 there were passes for everything: to get a job, to travel, even to stay out late at night.

White people, even children, gave out the passes, and they could ask to see them at any time. The black man hated the Pass Laws, but he soon learned to do what he was told. If not, he went to prison.

But in 1948, there was worse to come. It was called apartheid. It was the last move necessary to keep whites and blacks away from each other.

Blacks, whites and a new group called coloureds were to live in different parts of the cities and countryside. A coloured was someone with a family past that contained some blacks and some whites. People were listed not just by names and addresses, but by the colour of their skin. They were listed by race. Marriages between the races were unlawful.

But what do you do with black children who are as clever or cleverer than white children?

The white man had the answer to that too. Lessons for black children would be in Afrikaans, a language that was used nowhere else in the world. Teachers would tell black children that they could never be equal with whites. In this way, when a black child left school he was ready for his future.

Students march against lessons in Afrikaans, 1976

It was a future where he started at the bottom. The white man wanted to make sure he stayed there.

GOING TO WORK
1941–1943

IT WAS 1941. There was only one place for a bright young twenty-three year old to go. Johannesburg. It was everything that a capital city should be. Its buildings were tall, its streets were long and noisy, and its people were busy making money.

Work was not difficult to find. There was a war in Europe, and South Africa was helping to win it. It was just not the kind of work Nelson wanted to do. After all, he was a college man and the son of a Thembu Chief.

He was still angry about his journey to Johannesburg. He could only sit in a part of the train that showed a "NON EUROPEAN" sign. But when he reached Johannesburg, he could not believe how badly the city people felt about his black skin.

"I understand you need someone to work in the office," he said, to the manager of the Crown Mines.

The manager gave Nelson a long, hard stare. It was the look you might give to a cow at market. Slowly, the man's eyes travelled over Nelson's strong, young body. Nelson wanted to hit him.

"You can have the job of policeman," said the man. "Make sure those blacks do what they're told. Here's your stick."

"Stick!" It was not what Nelson had planned. But it was better than nothing, and much better than most jobs offered to blacks.

Within a few days the Chief discovered where his son was and ordered him home. When Nelson refused, the Chief spoke to the manager of the mines. In minutes Nelson was out of work. But he still refused to go home.

About this time, he met Walter Sisulu, son of a white father and a black mother. The older man welcomed the young Nelson to his home, where they talked about politics. They had a lot to say about what was wrong with the government. They soon became good friends. Walter gave Nelson his next job, selling homes. The pay was two pounds each month.

Nelson looked for somewhere to live. But he soon found out that black people and coloureds could not pick and choose. They could only live in places called townships. And one black township looked just like another. Matchbox houses, with no roads, no telephones, no electricity – and one lavatory and water pipe for forty people.

In conditions like these there was no family life. And often, because the men were so unhappy, they spent the little money they had at the beer hall. Too little food and too much drink led to arguing and fights. People broke the Pass Laws. And, of course, the police, who were never far away, took them to prison.

Out of two pounds, Nelson paid sixty-eight pence for his room and eighty-two pence for bus travel. That left fifty pence for a month's food.

"The people in the house were very good to me," he said. "They often waited for the sixty-eight pence and they always gave me a lovely free Sunday lunch."

One day, Nelson said to Walter, "There is only one way I can help my people. I need to learn about the law. I must become a lawyer."

"There was something about him, even then," Walter said, years later, when he and Nelson were famous. "I believed in him, and I gave him the money to study law. Then I found some white lawyers who agreed to let a black man work for them."

Nelson was a clever man, and he soon got a better job in the office. But this gave some of the white workers something to worry about.

One day Nelson was giving his secretary a letter to type when some white visitors walked in. The secretary's face became bright red and she stood up at once.

"Here you are, Nelson." She took a coin out of her bag and handed it to him. "Run down to the shop and bring me some soap to wash my hair." She didn't want the visitors to know she worked for a black man.

Nelson had a hard job not to laugh. And later that night when he told his friends, they all thought it was very funny.

But when the laughing was over, they talked for a long time. What kind of a country was it where this sort of thing could happen?

A FAMILY MAN
1944–1957

"I LOVED HIM the first time I saw him." Evelyn Ntoko Mandela is a lonely, grey-haired old lady. On her third finger she still wears the ring Nelson gave her on their marriage many years ago.

"He was so good-looking, had a wonderful smile, and we laughed a lot," says the first Mrs Mandela.

"Today, the whole world thinks he is some sort of god. But he's not. How can he be? He had other women, and he left his wife and children."

They got married in 1944. Evelyn was a cousin of Walter Sisulu. She was a nurse at the City Deep Mine Hospital. She and Nelson were very much in love, but the marriage got off to a poor start.

Nelson was studying and working part time. Evelyn's pay had to keep them both, and help with the expensive law lessons. Her sister gave them a room in her three-roomed house. But soon Evelyn discovered she was going to have a baby. Now, they had to look for a place of their own.

When Thembekile was born in 1947, they moved to a two-roomed house in Orlando, ten miles to the south-west of Johannesburg, and close to the Sisulus.

In those early days, Nelson was very much the family man. He liked shopping, bathing the baby and cooking. And as he became more successful, he planned all sorts of exciting things for his growing family.

"He was popular with all the children," said his second son, Makgatho, who was born in 1950. "And he was a wonderful story-teller."

But he was popular with women too. Too popular for the church-going Evelyn, who was very unhappy about Nelson's love-life. To her, marriage was about a promise made before God.

Nelson saw it differently. He didn't think it was wrong to take a lover. He liked beautiful women. He wanted to have other women and his marriage to Evelyn as well.

"It's my business," he told her. And then, angrily, "No policeman asks questions like you do."

But it was not just his love-life that caused trouble. Now his interest in politics began to cut into family time. Instead of taking the children to the cinema, and his wife to dances, he went to meetings. He filled his home with people who only talked about Pass Laws and unfairness to blacks.

"It wasn't the kind of life I wanted," said Evelyn. "But Nelson did, so I accepted it. Until the day I found him in our bedroom with another woman."

They argued angrily.

"It's our very own place," she told him. "If she doesn't leave, I shall throw hot water over her."

His answer was to walk out of the house and not come back. "We don't understand each other any more," he said.

But Evelyn was still in love with him, and she wanted to save the marriage. They tried again, but even the birth of a third son didn't bring them together.

They both knew the marriage was over the day Nelson seized her by the neck and shook her. "I'm leaving you," he exploded. "I don't love you any more."

The marriage was ended by law but Evelyn first heard about it through the newspapers. It was too late to do anything about it by then. Nelson was already seeing a lot of Winnie Madikizela.

To make enough money for herself and the children, Evelyn started a little store and worked a fifteen-hour day. She got up at four in the morning, and made baby clothes until she opened the shop at nine.

In 1962, when Nelson went to prison, Evelyn asked to see him, but he refused. Even so, her feelings remain the same. "I still think of myself as Nelson's wife," she says. "In the eyes of God, marriage is for ever."

POWER TO THE PEOPLE

"You'll make a very good lawyer," a friend at work told Nelson. "But stay out of politics. That's not for you."

How little the speaker knew. Nelson wanted to be a lawyer because he planned to do just that – go into politics. Black Africa needed people from all walks of life to help in its fight to be free.

At that time the voice of the people belonged to the ANC (African National Congress).

"God Save Africa" it sang as it carried its black, green and gold flags.

But there were few people to hear the song, and fewer still to see the flags. Hope was already dead in the heart of the black man. And the whites were not interested in the black man's song, flags or difficulties.

When Nelson joined the ANC in 1944, the war in Europe was coming to an end. He was certain that now there would be important changes for his people. But the battlefields, where black and white lived and died together, were soon forgotten. And in their place was the new enemy – apartheid.

"The ANC is a group of old men with nice, clean hands," Nelson told his friends Walter Sisulu and a man called Oliver Tambo, who was from Nelson's old college. "It's time for action. And I, for one, don't mind getting *my* hands dirty."

Together, they formed a group of young people, and called themselves the Youth League.

"Talking just isn't enough," the Youth League told the ANC. "Nobody is listening. Let's have a nation-wide stay-at-home-from-work day. No one will get hurt. But the whites will certainly feel the cold wind of change when they go to their banks."

Everybody agreed that it was a good idea. So they were not pleased when the Indian and Communist Parties also planned a stay-at-home day. It was to happen on May Day 1950 – just one month before the Youth League's action. Worst of all, it was being planned with the help of the ANC. "It will kill our action stone-dead," said Nelson angrily.

But he and the Youth League were interested to watch the success of the May Day stay-at-home. All day, the streets were crowded with men, women and children making their silent show of force. Nelson saw, too, how the day suddenly changed . . . How the air filled with the sounds of police guns, and women and children screaming . . . And how the ground grew red with their blood. Eighteen Africans were killed and more than thirty injured.

A march against apartheid, 1985

Nelson and Walter talked far into the night. "We need help," said Walter. "You saw what happened today. Those people stood alone. It's time for us all to join together."

Nelson didn't want to join with anybody else but he realised that, alone, they would lose in a fight against the power of the police. At last, he agreed. Years later, in court, in 1964, he said, "I am not a communist. I was never a communist. But when we, the black people, had no one, they were our friends."

The Youth League's first job after May Day

was to get more blacks to join the ANC. Their second job was to show that non-violent action *could* succeed. But to win they needed to be as brave as any soldier in battle.

It was Nelson's job to sell the idea. And not just in Johannesburg, but in the rest of South Africa, too.

NELSON ON TOUR
1951–1952

"WE NEED YOU. Will you join us?"

The same words, day after day, night after night. But the places were different and so, sometimes, were the answers.

The tour taught Nelson a lot. He saw what other parts of South Africa were really like. And he saw for himself the difficulties of people outside Johannesburg.

The journeys across country were long and tiring. Travel for the black man by bus and train was very uncomfortable. And when, at last, he arrived at a township, things were no better.

"A taxi? For you? You must be joking!"

"Where is the nearest hotel, then?" Nelson looked up and down the street.

"There are no hotels for blacks," said the taxi driver.

"A telephone?" said Nelson angrily.

"Townships don't have telephones. Get out of here, you dirty black."

It was a long way to the townships, through unlit streets where police waited at every corner. "Who are you?" they shouted. "What are you doing here at this time of night?"

Sometimes he had an address to go to. Sometimes he just chose a house and hoped for the best. Often the door was shut in his face. "Go away," they cried. "Can't you see we don't want you here?"

Not want him? Nelson couldn't believe it. They *needed* him and what he had to offer.

"You don't understand," they said, with their eyes on his dark city suit. "You don't know what it's like to live in fear. The police watch us all the time. They want us to break the law. Then they have an excuse to put us in prison. Some people disappear and never come back. You can't ask us to lose the little bit we have, for promises about the future."

But there were others who welcomed him with open arms. They wanted action, and they argued angrily about the idea of non-violence.

"We're not ready for anything else," Nelson told them. "We haven't the money or the guns. We haven't even got enough people ready to fight. And listen, my friends. If we fight, we're playing into the white man's hands. That's just what he wants us to do.

Then he'll destroy us. We *must* try a peaceful way first."

He smiled at their unhappy faces. "Non-violence isn't as easy as you might think. And it's not just staying at home, either. It's showing yourselves in the best possible way. You must wash yourselves and wear clean clothes. There must be no drinking or fighting. We want the government to see what we're really like."

It was the start. Doctors, teachers, lawyers, students and church men came forward now, ready for action. The ANC grew from seven thousand to one hundred thousand. At their first open meeting on 26 June 1950, Nelson took no notice of the Pass Laws, and talked on into the night. He and many others were put in prison.

But the peaceful action continued. Unable to stop it, the government put Mandela in prison for a second time. The prisons were full, but still the black man refused to fight. There was only one thing left for the government to do. Make trouble. Make it impossible for the blacks not to fight.

It was clever. It was nasty. But it worked. The police said that two black boys stole a pot of paint from a railway station and ran away. "We called to them to stop," one policeman said later. The boys went on running and were shot dead.

The black people went wild. Who cared about non-violent action now? Crowds of angry people raced through the township to the station. Eleven people died and twenty-seven were badly hurt.

Of course, the ANC knew the government caused the violence. The government stopped all meetings, and gave the police more power to force people to keep the Pass Laws.

But there was some success for Mandela, too. "What is this apartheid?" asked the rest of the world. The United Nations decided to take a long, hard look at conditions in South Africa.

For six months, Nelson Mandela could not leave Johannesburg or go to meetings. The government thought he was finished – out of business. The Youth League knew he was busier than ever.

MANDELA THE MAN

A WHITE SOUTH AFRICAN described Mandela: "I noticed people were turning and staring across the road . . . He was a head taller than anybody else, with a strong, healthy body that breathed power . . . Expensive clothes fitted beautifully, and he walked like a man who really believed in himself. Not just blacks, but whites too were looking. Even white women stopped and stared . . . And this in a country where black people counted for nothing."

There was, and is, something unusual about Nelson Mandela; something which makes him different from other people. Walter Sisulu recognised it the first time they met. "I knew that Nelson could and would help our people," he said.

A newspaper reporter recognised it, too. He wrote, *'He is one of the few men that both black and white can believe in'*. In 1990, many years later, he was proved right.

Mandela has always been a very healthy man. Even in his seventies, he gets up at sunrise and spends two hours getting into good shape. He walks, rides and bicycles. "A healthy body goes with a healthy mind," he says. In the early days of the troubles, people who met him could not believe what they saw. Here was a young man who lived where they lived, but he looked quite different. This smiling, bright-eyed man, exploding with good ideas, reached out to them and gave them new hope.

But he could be gentle too; a quietly understanding listener. He was never too tired. And, as time passed and he became famous, he was never too important.

He has a rich sense of fun. Not even the long, hard prison years on Robben Island stopped him laughing at himself or at life. Because he believed it was good for people to laugh, he often told jokes and funny stories.

Nelson at Wembley, London, in April 1990

And if they failed to amuse, he just used bad language to make them laugh.

Mandela is not one of the really great speakers of the age. When he addresses a meeting, he just says what he means. There is nothing very unusual about the way he says it. So why do people come in their thousands to listen? "It's not difficult to understand," says his great friend Oliver Tambo. "Nelson Mandela is a born leader."

NELSON WAS THIRTY-FIVE when he and Oliver Tambo went into business together. "Black lawyers, born of our land," said an excited friend. It was the day Nelson and Oliver moved furniture into a small office in Johannesburg and put up a sign outside.

They were a great team. Oliver was the quiet one, a thinker first and then a doer. Nelson was always part of the action. He thought quickly and put every thought to good effect at once.

In no time at all, everybody in the township knew about the two men. They knew, too, that they were much more than lawyers. Both men wanted the laws to be right and fair. And they cared deeply about the poor people who broke unfair laws.

There was certainly plenty of work. The prisons were full, with more prisoners in South Africa than in any other country in the world. And it was not hard to see why. There were so many reasons why a black person might go to prison. No land. No house. No job. No pass. All crimes in the eyes of the white man. It was even a crime to make, drink or sell beer. Women who tried to earn money for their hungry children in this way often ended up in prison.

And there were crimes born out of apartheid itself, crimes of hate. Some blacks –

men, women and children – searched the streets for trouble.

Long lines of people waited outside the offices of Mandela and Tambo. Inside, the two men wrote reports on the thousands of crimes that came before them. They had enough facts now: they could prove to the ANC that it was time for action.

Nelson really enjoyed working in the law office. He liked meeting people and helping them with their day-to-day difficulties. His work also took him into the law courts. It was a first for him and for the whites who were surprised to see a black lawyer. A few showed their fear and hate, but most accepted Nelson as a fellow lawyer. But he was not their equal.

"Oliver and I were black," he said. "And because of this, we had to be better than anybody else at our jobs. And even that was not enough. We soon realised that we could never reach the top. For that, you had to be white."

In court, Nelson was a powerful, exciting figure. Expert in using lawyer's language, he attacked with quick, clever questions. Often he amused the court, but it was to help him win and not just for fun.

The court room was full. All eyes followed the tall, young, black lawyer. For a moment, Nelson stared at the African house-boy who was in court for stealing clothes.

A rich, beautiful white woman sat at the

front of the court. Nelson noticed her expensive dress and hand-made shoes. He noticed, too, that the beautiful face was hard and the blue eyes cold. How is it possible, he wondered, for one person to have so much, and another to have so little?

He looked now at the clothes on a small table. His fingers ran through them, touching this one and then that. At last, he turned back to the room and held up some ladies underclothes. There was the sound of quiet laughter as he shook the panties for all to see.

Suddenly, he was looking at the woman again and holding out the panties in her direction. "Are these yours, Madam?"

The court room held its breath at the black man's daring. The woman's face became bright red, and she looked away from the panties. "No," she said, uncomfortably. "Certainly not!"

The hearing was over. Shortly afterwards, the government used another law to throw Nelson and Oliver out of their office. "It was lawful for us to work where we chose," said Nelson. "And we chose Johannesburg."

But the daytime office was closed, and they were forced instead to work at night and during the weekend.

"CONDITIONS WERE WORSE. Prices were rising. Bread, meat and vegetables were too expensive for black families. There was disease everywhere, the result of the black man's life. Young babies died at birth because their mothers worked too hard and ate too little.

The government offered nothing, not even for the sick and old. Instead, it sent out more and more spies. There were police spies, government spies, and those who spied on neighbours in return for a few pence.

Nelson brought in the Mandela Plan, an idea that would keep the people in touch. "We must continue to meet," he explained to ANC leaders. "But we must do it secretly and in small groups." They told each other about the meetings when they met in the street. They passed notes in the mines and on the buses. And when they met, it was always after dark and in somebody's home.

Secret meetings brought the people closer, and they listened with interest to the speakers. On a day to remember in June 1955, over three thousand people arrived, dressed in the ANC colours of gold, black and green. It was like a great birthday party. And they liked what they heard. "South Africa belongs to all the people, black and white. Everybody must be equal, at home, at work, at school and at play." All of this, they were told, would happen in an air of peace and friendliness.

Nobody noticed or recognised Nelson, at the back of the crowd. He was not supposed to be there, so he dressed up in old clothes. He was just glad to be a part of that important day. For once in their lives, his people were happy, excited and hopeful about the future. Only one thing worried him. There were too many police around; a silent police busy making notes and taking photographs.

The next day they came back, but this time they had guns and dogs. And this time they moved quickly through the crowd. They wrote down hundreds of names and addresses and took away any papers that looked important.

It marked the start of a police hunt that went on for months. During that time they took hundreds of people away. They came for Nelson in December 1956. He and his family were in bed when they came. "Daddy! Daddy!" his children screamed when the police forced their way into the bedroom.

"Don't be afraid," Nelson comforted, while the police searched his house and broke his furniture. Rough hands pulled him away from the children.

"You're coming with us," he was told. "Hurry up and get your things together."

"Go back to bed," Nelson told the unhappy Evelyn and their children. "Everything will be all right. You'll see."

But everything was not all right. One hundred and fifty-five people were taken away that night. One hundred and fifty-five people were thrown into prison. "DON'T FEED!" said the sign on the door. Their crime? Attacking the government!

THE SECOND MRS MANDELA

"NOT THAT ANC MANDELA!" Hilda Madikizela looked up from the photograph to her step-daughter. The answer was on Winnie's face. "Are you out of your mind? I'm telling you, Winnie, this man will go to prison and stay there."

Winnie's father said the same, and more. "You're too young. End it now, before you get hurt."

"I love him."

"Love!" her father repeated. "What do you know about love? And what does he? He's got a wife. And children, too! Will you love them – and the unkind things people will say about you . . . ? There'll be talk – lots of it. This man is famous and he's supposed to set an example."

It was all right for an African man to have

four wives, thought Winnie, but not to walk away from one.

"Winnie? She was a pretty lady," remembered Makgatho, Nelson's second son from his first marriage. "She laughed a lot and was very friendly. Then Daddy said she was going to be our new mother . . . It seemed strange at the time, because we already had a mother. But I liked her and, after their marriage, I often visited them."

The first time Winnie saw Nelson was in court. "He was a most exciting man. I just couldn't take my eyes off him," she said.

Then they met in a shop in Johannesburg. Nelson was alone, and Winnie was with Oliver Tambo and his girlfriend, Adelaide.

"My heart jumped when he smiled," said Winnie. "But I never thought he would really look at me . . . He was famous. I was nobody."

But, within days, Nelson telephoned the nobody and asked her out for lunch.

"It was wonderful and terrible at the same time," said Winnie. "I wanted to go, but I was afraid, too. He was a man of the world and he knew everything. I was just out of college and I knew nothing – not even which clothes to wear. The restaurant was full. Everybody looked at us. I wondered what they thought about me – I was even wearing my friend's best dress! Nelson said it was very pretty. Suddenly, I realised he really wanted me there, and I began to feel more comfortable."

Winnie Madikizela was twenty-two.

Nelson Mandela was thirty-eight. They fell in love.

"But he was never really mine," she said. "He belonged to the people. I would always be second best. But I loved him wildly and I knew that he loved me too, in his way."

She was not understanding at all when it came to other women. "I knew all about his women," she said. "And I wasn't having any of that. What I have is mine – and mine alone."

Nelson described what happened the day Winnie caught him with the secretary of a visitor. "She took one look at the woman, who was very beautiful, then she seized me round the neck. Remember, we weren't married and I was a very strong man. But I was weak against the power of her anger."

Winnie was her father's third unwanted daughter. A tall, strong child, she played violent games and took her beatings like a boy. Because she was bright, her father sent her away to school. She learned quickly, but not just from books.

She was tall for her age, a beautiful girl who looked very sexy. Men, as well as boys, desired her, and offered her money to go to bed with them. "I dared not tell my father or my teacher," she said. "They would never believe I wasn't a bad girl."

At the Hofmeyer School of Social Work she learned about the conditions in the black townships. "I wasn't ready for what I found,"

Nelson and Winnie marry on 14 June 1958

she said. "Mothers and young babies slept in empty boxes in the streets. They had no food, no money and no one to care if they lived or died."

Her work with the poor brought her closer still to Nelson. And soon he took her to meet his friends. "Those were happy days," she said. "We sat around eating, drinking, and talking. Colour didn't matter. We were all friends, black and white. One day, Nelson mentioned a friend who would make me a wedding-dress. Suddenly I realised he was asking me to marry him . . . Nelson was given a six-day pass for the marriage which was held at my home in June 1958. Not nearly enough time to visit his family, as well as mine. So I kept part of the cake for the day when Nelson would be truly free and we could go to his family together. I waited over twenty years for that day to come."

Winnie added two rooms to Nelson's Orlando home, and she made a garden from the dirt at the back. It was a lonely start for the young wife. Nelson was busy with the ANC and the law business. When he was home, he liked to fill the house with friends. "Money is supposed to go round," he said, and he made sure it did. He never drank beer himself, but there was always plenty for others, plenty to drink and eat.

Winnie returned to work. "We needed the money," she said. But there was another reason. "Now I was not Winnie Mandela," she said. "I was Nelson Mandela's wife, and I walked in his shadow."

She joined the ANC and marched against Pass Laws for women. "When our men go out in the morning, we never know if they'll return. What will happen to our children if these same Pass Laws are used against us?"

Winnie was put in prison. "They took away our clothes and searched us. There were two thousand of us crowded together with dirty blankets for beds, and no lavatories – only buckets that soon filled up."

It was a month before the ANC paid to get them out of prison. A whole month before Nelson could take home his young wife, who was going to have their first child.

IN COURT
1956–1960

FROM THE NIGHT IN 1956, when the police took Nelson away, it was nearly five years before the government was ready to bring him to court. He was not kept in prison for that time, but was forced to keep the Pass Laws and was watched all the time. During those five years, Nelson left Evelyn, married Winnie and had two daughters.

In court, it was agreed at last that the ANC were not communists. Fifty-nine were freed. The rest were still held because of their attacks on the government. Nelson asked the government to meet the ANC for talks. But, even as he spoke, he feared it was too late. The people wanted action. And they wanted it now.

It started on 21 March 1960, in Sharpeville, a black township where the people were the poorest of the poor. When they heard about an action march, they decided to join. And why not? After all, they had nothing to lose. Two thousand left their passes at home and marched in silence to the police station.

For the first time, the government was unsure of itself. The face of Africa was changing. And the world was talking about not buying things with South African labels. A quiet march in Sharpeville suddenly seemed to have much more importance.

Aeroplanes circled the sky, and hundreds of police were brought in to fight the silent crowd. They shot sixty-nine men, women and children.

While an angry world watched the Sharpeville murders on television, trouble was just beginning in Langa, near Cape Town. Ten thousand people went on another action march. They were angry about the crowded buildings where men were forced to live away from their wives and children. Police killed two and injured forty-nine.

As a result of Sharpeville and Langa, the black people got ready for more action against the government. There were stay-at-home days, marches and fights. ANC leaders openly burned their passes.

Mandela and other ANC leaders were taken from their homes and put in prison. Nelson's lawyers refused to continue helping him in court in such troubled times.

Now Nelson had to act for himself. On a dirty prison blanket, he studied the hundreds of pages he needed for court. At the end of it all, the court failed to prove anything against him. Nelson and the other ANC leaders were free.

NELSON WENT HOME to Winnie and their two daughters, but not for long. He had decided to go into hiding.

"Get some things together, Winnie," he said. "In a day or two, I'll be going away for a very long time. You mustn't worry. Friends will look after you and bring you news."

"I couldn't believe it," she said. "We were supposed to be a family . . . I was afraid of a life without Nelson."

"Please, please, don't forget us," she cried. "Promise to think of me and the children sometimes."

Nelson became angry. "How dare you!" he shouted. "This is my business, and I don't need you to tell me what to do."

In *his* business there was certainly no place for Winnie and the children. But, at least, he paid the bills for six months before he went, and sent round friends to help.

"I knew that it was time for me to stand up for what I believed," he said later. "I knew, too, that Winnie and the children would pay the price. But somebody had to do it. And I was sure that the somebody ought to be me." It never crossed his mind to ask Winnie how *she* felt. It was many years before he really understood the effect of his action on her and the children.

Nelson's new job was to lead a group for national action. Within days, he was once again a wanted man, with police everywhere looking for him.

He disappeared from sight. He travelled by night, and never stayed more than twenty-four hours in any one place. He had secret meetings by day, but kept a watchful eye out for black spies who would report him.

It was a dangerous life, but it had its funny side, too. Nelson loved dressing up and fooling the police. He cleaned windows, brushed streets, worked in a garage, and became driver to a rich, white friend. It was like an exciting adventure story. But the good guy was only a man, and the bad guy was a whole government. And while many people enjoyed the fun, there were those who saw it differently. This was no game, this was about life and death. And not just Nelson's life, either, but the lives of everybody who helped him.

It was twenty years since the ANC started its non-violent action. Everybody agreed that it was not working. But Nelson was afraid of the next step. Violent action would bring the full force of the government against the black people.

In one last try to keep the peace, he called for a three-day stay-at-home from 29 May 1961. Then he wrote to the government. '*It's still not too late. But now we either talk it out or shoot it out.*' The government's answer was to set up army camps and hand out guns. They filled the black townships with police and soldiers, and they taught white women to shoot.

The stay-at-home failed. With the full power of the South African government against them, it was not surprising. At least, it forced the ANC to decide its next move. Nelson was told, "Start a fighting group. But take only necessary action, and make sure there is no loss of life."

Nelson was at the top of the government's list of wanted men. Every day might be his last. Now, he faced the terrible fact that he might never see Winnie or the children again. He realised he would do anything – take any chance – just to hear her voice or see her smile.

One day, she received word to drive to a street corner garage. A workman in a blue coat and trousers jumped into the car. "I understand you're having trouble with the engine," he shouted, as Winnie moved out of the driving seat. "Keep looking ahead." Nelson spoke quietly now, and drove out into the traffic. "And don't smile!"

"I dared not smile, and I was almost too happy to speak. I tried to tell him about the children. But it was all too quick – there was no time. He drove round a few streets and then took me back to the garage. He bought me a new car, and then just disappeared into the crowds."

Shortly after this in January 1962, the ANC got Mandela out of the country. For the first time, he went to the free world. He visited countries where he was just another man, not a black man. He saw blacks and whites all living freely together. When he returned home, he knew how to make war on his enemies. He had money for guns. And he had hope in his heart.

In Orlando, the police were visiting Winnie almost daily. "Where is your husband?" they shouted, as they marched through the house in their search for addresses.

"I don't know," she said, with her arms around her children. It was true. For weeks, she had no idea where Nelson was or what he was doing. At that time, he was living in a shed on a white friend's farm. There, he taught a small group about the art of modern war. It would be their job to travel about the country, and destroy important government buildings.

With great difficulty his white friends brought the Mandela children to the farm for a week. They played games and swam every day with Nelson in the pool. Winnie came too, but dared to stay for only one night.

Nelson was caught quite suddenly and when he was least ready. He was driving his white friend when the car was stopped by two police cars.

"I hid my gun and notebook," said Nelson. "I told them I was a driver and my name was

David Motsamai. But it was no use, they were very sure of themselves. I wondered later why they were on that quiet road at that time of day ... I think somebody helped them."

He knew he would go to prison. He knew it would be for a few years. But neither he nor Winnie thought they would be grandparents by the time he came out.

"LIFE"
1964

"AN HOUR WAS LIKE A YEAR. I had nothing to read, nothing to write, nothing to do. And worse, I had no one to speak to. And all this because I refused to wear prison clothes and eat their terrible food. I was a fool to try to beat them. It was a battle they were certain to win. They knew I needed work to do and people to talk to. So I put on the shirt and short trousers, and I forced myself to eat the food. Now I was busy again. I made mail bags, and I was able to talk to people.

The long wait in prison was at last over, and the court case was ready to begin.

Because he left the country without a pass and led the action days, he went to prison for five years. Nelson was not surprised. Winnie could not believe it. Five years seemed like a lifetime.

Within two years, Nelson was back in court. This time he had to pay the price for attacking the government and for destroying its buildings.

The effects of prison life were showing on Nelson. He looked old, tired and too thin, and his skin was an unhealthy, grey colour. But the smile was still there, the lifted hand sign and the voice as strong as ever. Very soon, because conditions were better during the court case, he looked like the Nelson everyone remembered.

This time, he was his own lawyer. It gave him what he wanted – a stage – and from it he could speak to the world. He spoke about conditions in the townships. He talked about apartheid and the unfair Pass Laws. He wanted black people to have a voice in choosing a government.

"What I did was not from a love of violence," he told the court. "It was because the government refused to listen to peaceful action."

Brave words! But they failed to excuse his crimes against the government. Crimes he knew he could pay for with his life.

Outside the court, the crowds waited for hours to hear if Nelson would die. Inside, Nelson talked with Walter Sisulu. "If I'm going to die," Nelson told him, "I shall ask for nothing except the chance to speak." Both men got "life". The government didn't want any dead, black gods.

Three days later, Nelson's action group blew out the front of the Post Office in Johannesburg.

Report in a British Sunday Newspaper 1964

'Many people will feel strongly about the news that Mandela and others will go to prison for life.

'But there is a kind of war in South Africa. These men worked against the government and they were caught.

'Today, the South African government is pleased to see the last of Nelson Mandela. In ten years' time it may be equally pleased that he is still alive. With him as go-between, they may have a chance to put the new thinking into action.'

ROBBEN ISLAND
1964–1982

"THEY SENT US TO PRISON so that the world would forget us," said Nelson. "They believed that the conditions would destroy us. They thought that we would never again be strong or brave enough to fight for any cause.

"They failed because we were not just prisoners, we were black prisoners. Every day, *they* remembered it – and so did *we*. The battle was still on.

"My first job was to fight for some very necessary changes. More food. Warm blankets. Chairs and tables. And then, we needed the chance to work, to speak, and to look after our health."

"Nelson taught me how to go on living," one man said. "When I was ill, he came to see me. He even cleaned my lavatory."

"We were watched," said Nelson. "Powerful men marched up and down with big dogs. They counted us out in the morning and back in at night. They took away our clothes and searched our cold bodies. They stole our food and sold it. The lights were kept on all night. And the letters which came every six months were often held back. Then, slowly, condi-

Nelson with Walter Sisulu in Robben Island prison, 1966

Prisoners break rocks and make mailbags on Robben Island

tions got better. We were given fresh clothes, clean blankets, hot water, tables and chairs, and better food. There was plenty of work to keep us busy during the day, and at night we studied."

As the years passed, Robben Island changed – together with prisons all over the world. There were films to watch, records to listen to, and games like cards and table tennis to play.

Robben or Seal Island is a cold, rocky island seven miles north-west of Cape Town. It is very hot in summer and terribly cold in winter. There is plenty of wild life and, across the water, you can see the beauty of Table Mountain.

Nelson continued to get up at sunrise and, to keep himself healthy, he always chose the hardest jobs on the island. He broke rocks for a new prison building. He dug until his back bent, his hands burned, and his eyes were red with dry dust. In winter, he picked sea plants from the ice-cold waters of the South Atlantic.

His six-monthly letters mostly came on time. It was not the same with visits because Winnie was often in prison herself. Somehow, the years passed.

LIFE WITHOUT NELSON
1964–1990

"When Nelson went to prison," Winnie said, "I didn't know where to turn or what to do. Every time I opened my mouth, the newspapers were full of 'Mandela's Wife Says...' In their eyes, *I* was the voice of the ANC. And I knew so little about politics! I was a wife and mother. And suddenly, I had no husband and my two little girls had no father. I learned to hate."

The happy, open-hearted girl who married Nelson changed into a woman of steel.

Zindzi was six. "Mummy, you say Daddy is in prison because he's fighting for us," she said, one day. "But next door, their Daddy is at home. Why is my Daddy in prison and not theirs?"

There was nothing Winnie could do for Nelson or the other leaders. "But I could do something to help their wives and families," she said.

But helping these people was against the law! In the middle of the night, the police came and took her away.

She was kept in a small prison, with a bucket for a lavatory, and a light that never went out. "For hours every day, I walked up and down. I talked all the time. I talked to Nelson, to the children, to a fly on the wall."

They asked her questions for five days and nights. Her skin changed colour, and her heartbeat quickened until she was sure she was going to die. "I have a heart condition," she said.

"Then tell us something useful before you disappear," shouted her questioner. "You know too much to die."

In the end, she agreed with everything they said. "I knew nothing. But everywhere there was the sound of people screaming. I had to stop it. So, I said yes to everything."

She spent the next sixteen months alone. When they let her go, she had to remain inside her house and couldn't have any visitors.

"After two years, they let me visit Nelson. I spent days thinking about it, and wondering what to wear. I wanted to leave him with something beautiful to remember in the long, lonely days ahead.

"We spoke down a telephone and stared at each other through a small, dirty window.

There was such a lot I wanted to say, but there was always somebody listening. Most of all, I wanted to touch him, to feel his hand in mine."

The years passed. Nelson was still in prison, and the little girls grew up. It was in Winnie's nature to be a fighter, so she joined a group that worked for the equality of black women. In law, black women were like children: they had no voice. When a black woman's husband died, she lost her home as well as her husband.

When Andrew Young, a black American from the United Nations, came to Soweto where Winnie lived, the government moved her out of her home. They feared she would talk too much. They didn't want Young to interest himself in black ways of thinking, or in schoolchildren who hated their lessons in Afrikaans.

They drove her to a white town, Brandfort, where no one spoke her language. "My house was three rooms, all filled with stones and dirt," said Winnie. There was no water, electricity or lavatory. But, worst of all, after the move our daughter, Zindzi, became ill."

Winnie decided to fight back. "The blacks had a beer hall and one shop," she said, "The whites had everything." Trouble broke out when Winnie went shopping in white Brandfort. The police were called as she marched in and out of food stores, dress shops and the post office. "I thought it was sad," she said.

"*They* were afraid of *me!*"

But she was angry when the police came for her because she wore a green, gold and black dress – ANC colours, they said. "But I like those colours," she told them. "They suit me."

Another day, she was in trouble because she talked to two people at once. "I wanted to buy some wood for the fire," she said. "And then somebody joined us with a chicken to sell."

"It's a meeting!" shouted the police. "It's a meeting!"

Slowly, the whites accepted her. And the blacks began to copy her success. They made gardens and planted seeds. They even used 'white' telephones and bread shops. But her life in Brandfort ended suddenly the day her house was destroyed during a children's action march.

Winnie returned to Soweto. It was against the law, but the eyes of the world were on South Africa. Its government decided to take no action against the wife of Nelson Mandela.

In Johannesburg, she opened the Mandela Family Office, and took her place on the stage at ANC meetings. Like Nelson, all those years before, she knew it was time to fight her own battle to be free.

NEW FACES
1970–1980

FROM HIS LONELY PRISON on Robben Island, Mandela watched the changing face of the black troubles. He was not supposed to know anything about the outside world, but somehow the news got through.

The ANC was losing power, and a new thinking was taking its place. Different kinds of people were leading the action now – young people from universities, colleges, and schools. Students and schoolchildren joined together against the idea of separate schools. Their voices were young and unafraid. They refused to live in the white man's shadow. They were black and glad of it.

Hundreds of teachers walked out of their jobs. Thousands of children refused to go to school. The blood bath that followed shook the world.

Students and schoolchildren march in Cape Town

On 16 June 1976, a crowd of excited schoolchildren marched against learning lessons in Afrikaans. The police turned their guns on them.

On Robben Island, the hot water was suddenly cut off. Nelson knew at once that there was trouble. But it was some days before he heard the news of the black children's battle.

Over the next sixteen months, hundreds of children were murdered. Hundreds disappeared. And thousands were injured for life.

Steve Biko was one of the many students who believed in the new thinking. His violent death in September 1977, at the hands of the South African police will never be forgotten.

WHEN WILL MANDELA SING?
1982

PRESIDENT BOTHA came to power in 1978. He talked about blacks and whites being good neighbours and tried not to mention apartheid. It was a cover up for a new grouping of black people. The government needed blacks who had money. It wanted them to start businesses and to own houses. In return, it promised to open some white hotels and restaurants to them.

From prison, Nelson managed to send a few words to his followers. *'Apartheid has failed,'* he wrote. *'But it is not the time for new groups. We must keep black people in all walks of life together. The world is with us. Success is certain.'*

Black newspapers pressed the government to free Mandela. They reported talks with Nelson's daughter, Zindzi. "Let my father go," she cried. The government made a list of Nelson's crimes. "In prison, 'Life' means life," they said.

Suddenly and without reason, they moved Nelson and Walter Sisulu to Pollsmoor Prison, just outside Cape Town. Conditions were better than on Robben Island. There was more fresh food, and there were more radios and newspapers. But the walls were high, there was nowhere to walk, and no beautiful Table Mountain to look at. And they missed the friends of those eighteen years on the island. Nelson even missed the loneliness of his prison and the long, peaceful hours of study.

But the visits were wonderful. After all those years he could really see Winnie and talk to her without a telephone. He broke prison rules and told her about conditions in Pollsmoor. "It's unhealthy here," he said. "Water is coming in through the walls. I'm having trouble with my foot because my shoes are too small. We all must see a doctor, and soon."

These were not the kind of stories the government wanted Winnie to broadcast. Soon after this, they let Nelson have his first real visit. They wished to prove to the world that he was in good health.

"It's impossible to describe my parents' feelings," said Zindzi. "Remember, it was twenty-two years since they touched or kissed or held each other."

It was the beginning of other visits. Britain's Lord Bethell, who worked for years to free Mandela, described their first meeting. "I saw a tall man with silver hair in a dark green shirt and blue trousers. We shook hands. 'You must be one of Winston Churchill's family,' he laughed, looking at my round, heavy body. It was a surprising visit. I expected to give him some comfort, but it was not like that at all. I was his visitor, and *he* looked after *me*. He told me about Robben Island and showed me his garden – oil containers full of fruit and vegetables . . . Of course, he had lots of questions about the world and world leaders. But I couldn't believe how much he already knew – how up-to-date he was . . . As I see it, the difficulty in Pollsmoor is not about conditions, but why he is still there . . . Twenty-one years in prison for destroying some buildings!"

Different visitors had different ideas. One said Mandela was like a head of government.

Another said he was still a man of violence. But on one thing all the visitors agreed: "Free Mandela Now!"

"It isn't the South African government that is keeping Mr Mandela in prison," Botha told the country. "It is himself. He must promise not to plan or join any violent action against the government."

Nelson's answer was read by Zindzi to a crowd of more than ten thousand people. *'Let President Botha stop his own violence. Let him speak out against apartheid. Too many have died. I cannot and will not make promises when I, and you – the people – are not free. Prisoners cannot make promises. Only free men can do that.'*

Three years later in 1988, he reached his seventieth birthday. "Free Mandela," cried the world as seventy-five thousand people in London's Wembley Stadium sang, "Happy Birthday, Mandela." Hundreds of thousands of cards arrived at Pollsmoor Prison, and everywhere there was the feeling of a holiday. Everywhere except Soweto, Nelson's old home. There, the police were out in force. Everything was stopped: football matches, music, film shows and Mandela birthday parties. But they were not quick enough to stop hundreds of balloons filling the sky with ANC colours.

MANDELA FREE
February II 1990

NELSON SPENT THE LAST few years in Pollsmoor prison alone. 'Out of sight, but much in mind' said one newspaper. He was in President Botha's mind a lot. He moved Nelson into a little house with its own office and telephone. He could now swim, ride a bike and cook his own meals.

On his seventy-first birthday, his family came to visit. They were all there – children, grandchildren and great-grandchildren.

His oldest daughter, Maki, wrote, *'He was almost as I remembered him. He spoke to each of us. The children knew about their grandfather from lessons in school . . . It was a comfortable house with a fire and television room. The dining-room table was full of meats, vegetables, fruit, and lovely sweet cakes . . . Later, Daddy went into the kitchen and made hot chocolate for all the children.'*

That same year, the government began to talk about freeing Nelson. And because it suited them now, they called him "leader".

There were twenty-eight million blacks in South Africa, and sixty per cent of the country's riches was black money.

Separate schooling failed. Apartheid was failing. Black power was growing. More and more black students were coming out of colleges and asking for higher pay – and getting it. The government was worried now about how long the black people would continue paying the country's bills. It was their money which kept the army and police in business. In return, they got trouble.

Mandela was the government's only hope. He alone could keep the black people together. But they feared, too, what might happen when he was free. "We must choose the right time," they said.

"My conditions must be met," Nelson told them. "All ANC leaders must be free, and there will be no promises about the future. I shall accept nothing else."

In 1989, there was talk of a date in November and December, but both passed. And then, on 2 February 1990, President de Klerk surprised the world. "It is time for change," he said. "Time for new thinking. ANC leaders will be free." On 11 February 1990, Nelson Mandela, hand in hand with Winnie, walked out into the sunshine.

They were driven away in a silver BMW with four police cars to look after them. They travelled through streets crowded with singing, dancing people. Fifty thousand people were waiting at a sports field to welcome them.

Reporters loved him. "He's a natural," they said. Mandela went to prison while America's President Kennedy was alive, and before South Africa had television. But he loved cameras and did nine news reports, one after

Nelson and Winnie walk out into the sunshine, 11 February 1990

another. In all of them, he spoke well of President de Klerk. But he made no secret of the fact that the fight against apartheid would continue.

Everywhere, right across the world, people wanted to see him. His three-day visit to New York cost that city over four million dollars.

To Nelson, the six-weeks tour of fourteen nations was necessary. "We want the world to go on refusing to buy South African things," he said. "And we need lots of money – at least twenty million pounds – to turn the ANC into a recognized party. And we need schools and hospitals and trucks and telephones and bicycles."

The world continued to buy South African things as world leaders all agreed it was time to help South Africa, not make life more difficult. But Nelson got his money; well beyond his twenty million.

There were Mandela cups and coins and

Nelson shakes hands with President de Klerk, May 1990

coats and hats and T-shirts and pictures and videos. But the rich wanted more than cups and T-shirts; they wanted to reach the man himself. It cost six hundred pounds to have a drink with him. Fifteen hundred pounds was the price of a talk. For three thousand pounds, you could sit with him at his table and eat his food.

Of course, there were those who thought the tour was just a nasty money-maker. And there were others who worried about what that twenty million pounds would be used for. Everybody knew that Mandela would take any action that was necessary to free black Africa.

THE FUTURE

WHEN THE EXCITING DAYS of the tour were over, Nelson faced the future. He knew that many people, blacks and whites, were waiting for him to take action. But there were difficulties. For one thing, the ANC was not ready. Its leaders were returning from prison and from other parts of the world. The party itself needed time to change its thinking. Yesterday's enemy was suddenly today's friend. Some people said that too many died for that to be possible.

When Nelson Mandela walked free from prison, people thought he would bring peace to South Africa. But now, over a year later, that dream seems to be disappearing. The blacks are at war with themselves – ANC against Zulu. The police that stormed the streets to keep apartheid laws now try to stop black killing black.

One thing is certain, Nelson will go on fighting. He says, "To stop now would be a mistake that our children's children would not forget. We must not let fear stand in our way."